Law of Attraction Planner & Workbook

Aria Edwards

DEDICATION

This book is dedicated to you, who seeks greater understanding of the universal powers around you in order to create higher understanding and mastery of the great natural Law of Attraction. You've been manifesting and attracting your entire life without know it. Now is *your* time to attract all of the greatness available to you as soon as you learn to use your thoughts to create your reality.

Welcome

You've been turned on to all that the Law of Attraction can manifest for you and you've heard countless real life rags-to-riches stories crediting this ultra-powerful universal force. Now it's your turn, but where do you begin?

I have manifested everything from cars and furniture to cash and love using the powerful forces of the very real Law of Attraction. I didn't do it right way. It took years for me to understand the laws enough to have the faith in them and take the leap. Once I was ready, I literally dove in and absolutely amazing things happened.

It took hitting rock bottom to inspire me to dive-in and make these principals really work for me. That's often it works because it takes a *burning desire* and a true *change in the way you think and react* to the world around you to make the big changes most of us need to use the Law of Attraction.

There's a lot to learn and it takes *dedication*. It took true dedication and downright *obsession* for me to achieve this, and I couldn't find any affordable step-by-step guides to get me into the practice and abundance mindset I wanted and needed.

In these pages, you'll find a space for the daily exercises I used to manifest over $100,000 in my first six months of manifestation lifestyle.

Yes, it takes work. However, I believe that like me, you will find that working on your own life is much more rewarding spiritually, mentally, and financially when you learn to attract your greatest *desires*.

Use this guided <u>Law of Attraction planner</u> to become a *money magnet*!

How-To Use

The first step in putting the Law of Attraction to work for you is creating *positive energy* and vibrations. It may sound like hokey, new-age mumbo-jumbo, but *like attracts like*. If you want a beautiful, positive, abundant life, you need to start be creating this energy.

The study of Quantum Physics has demonstrated that we, along with everything else around us, are made up of energy. The cells in our body, the molecules and atoms that make up those cells, and so on into smaller and smaller building blocks of life, the universe, and everything, is in its most basic essence, *energy*.

This is why in modern experiments where plants or fruit is subjected to either abuse or loving care, the loving care group always flourishes while the abuse group rots and fades away.

Step one in becoming a *Master Manifestor* is to create great energy around yourself through your attitudes and actions. For most of us, this takes time, practice, and careful attention. For the best results, you need to regularly create this positive space for positive reflection and goal-setting.

I started with an old notebook and massive debt. That tattered notebook evolved into the organized sections of this workbook. My exhausted energy and beat-down attitude evolved into a predominantly abundant mental attitude and money in the bank.

This guided workbook contains a sample worksheet in addition to 60 day's worth of worksheets (plus an extra 5, just in case!). In 60 days, you should at least start to see grand changes in your life.

This guide is in hard copy because there is something about writing down your intentions, goals, affirmations, and things you are grateful for that really cements them energetically. I love the convenience of everything digital, but have found that taking the time and space to work by hand amplifies the power of the Law of Attraction.

This guide works well in conjunction with an effort to continue to explore the law of attraction when it becomes a daily habit. Don't feel pressured to fill out an entire page in one sitting, however. This workbook works best when you spend a bit of time on it throughout the day.

Start with your daily intentions in the morning and then get organized and inspired for the day with making your list of action items. Make it a part of your routine to get through the affirmations section by lunch and complete the gratitude and forgiveness sections at the end of the day in a moment of quiet reflection.

Date

Date each entry. This is extremely helpful to keep yourself accountable and on track. It's also very rewarding to look back over the months and see how far you've come. There's another positive vibration amping up your *intention* to *have your dreams*.

Daily Intentions

First thing in your day (and it is, *your* day), before you start returning emails and making appointments, show the universe that *you* are important (and worth the positive energy) by setting aside a moment of reflection on what you'd like to accomplish that day. You may find that these are similar at first. As you move through your own personal manifestation journey, your daily intentions should evolve and feel more natural.

Keep your intentions *positive and productive*. After all, this is how you'd like your day to go, right?

Think… What sort of day would you like to have? What are your priorities today? In what ways will you be creating a positive space and environment for yourself today? What are you *doing today* to achieve your dreams?

Six Most Important Action Items

Great entrepreneurs including Charles Schwab & Mary Kay Ash have found something special about a list of the *six* most important things to do. There is something about this number that is small enough that it is ultra-manageable, but large enough that you can feel accomplished after accomplishing each item on this list.

This list should include items that need to get done to keep them from bogging down your energy as well as self-care items since these are important to keeping your energy flowing.

It's part to-do list, part action energy list. These are the items you need to tackle *first* in order to maintain your daily intentions. Start with must-do items, and then fill in items that will amp up your manifesting muscle by de-cluttering and caring for your environment and even your body.

Be sure to have at least one self-care item on your list each day as well as action items for achieving business or career goals.

I Specifically Want

This is where you put in your order with the universe. It gets your energy vibrating at the level of what it is that you *desire* in order to attract these desires.

Your desires will evolve and change, and you'll find that those items most important to you will appear most often. These things that you are spending the most mental energy on are the things that you will attract with the most force.

Be specific with your desires. Really zero-in on the *what* (but not the how) and ask, believe, receive. Often, what we desire is delivered in an unexpected way. That's why those who decide to finally *enjoy* single life after years of looking for a soul mate find love and those put having a baby on hold find themselves pregnant by *happy accident*. Peace and happiness vibrations are the most important components in manifesting your desires, the ideas of how just gets in the way. What Master Manifestors have learned is that the *how* Boggs down the *what*.

Who is it that you want to be? Write this down each day, allow it to evolve as necessary, and then *be* the person in your dreams each and every day. Do you have a career goal? How does it feel to be this person?

Take it a step further with what you want to do. Do you want to travel? What are the things you would be doing if you had manifested the dream already?

What do you *have* in the life of your dreams? What do you truly want to receive? What do you desire most? Is it a specific income level? Your dream home?

How I Will Feel When I Have It

Let this Law of Attraction order dictate your *predominant mental attitude*. How does financial freedom, your dream car, that gorgeous home make you *feel?* This step is really important because emotions and feelings have a stronger vibration than thoughts.

Think of what you want. *Feel* how it will feel when you have it. Act out of the happiness and joy that having it today.

Affirmations

Law of Attraction practitioners talk about affirmations because they work. You need to not only start a vibration with that order of what you want and how it will feel when you have it, you also need to keep that energy flowing to speed up your results.

Affirmations are a great way to do this because you can use them throughout the day either in your head or out-loud. You can *repeat* them in your head while you brush your teeth or while you wait on an appointment. You can say them out-loud in the shower or in the car while you wait for a traffic light to change.

Take a look at your *attitudes* and think about what needs help. If you feel broke, your affirmations should guide you to a feeling of wealth. If you feel ill, your affirmations should guide you to a feeling of health.

An income level is a simple affirmation that once practiced becomes highly effective. Start at a level believable for you, whether it's just a few hundred dollars extra each month, $3000/month, $10,000/month, or $100,000/month and adjust as you manifest this amount.

You may be manifesting money that you didn't even notice, so use the back section of this book (or the free digital version available at www.goldenintuition.com) to track the money that comes into your life. At a point, I realized that I wasn't attracting more money because I was actually achieving that income level without even realizing it once I counted things I was selling on eBay and Etsy. I changed my income affirmation and that month my income skyrocketed!

This feeds into the gratitude section because appreciating what you have creates great positive energy.

Gratitude

Gratitude is one of those things that seems very simple, but really isn't at all. You've likely heard of a gratitude journal before, even Oprah swears by them. This section of your daily worksheet has amazing powers to put your energy in line with receiving greatness.

Sure, who wouldn't love a nicer home, but take a look around you and remember that your home is a dream home to millions of people around the world. Appreciating the home you have creates a great energy, letting the Law of Attraction create a flow of positive "I *love* my home" energy.

The same is true for family, whatever time you do have for yourself on a busy day, anything. Appreciating what you have opens doors to improving that area of your life.

Some days, it truly is a daunting task to come up with 6 things to be grateful for. Look deep, you'll find them. I've literally had "wine" on my list multiple times. Some days, you just need to be thankful that you're alive and have a new day on the horizon that that's okay. You're still working in a space of shunning negative energy in favor of positive energy.

I Honestly Forgive

Creating positive energy through gratitude, affirmations, and intentions is part of the puzzle. It's also very important to clear out negative energy. I go into more detail about de-cluttering both mentally and physically in other Golden Intuition resources, but it is important to do something daily.

In order to really get the law of attraction working for you, you need to clean out your closets and de-clutter the rooms in your home. This *frees up* so much *energy* that although it can feel like a daunting task, it will leave you feeling much lighter and *clarified* once it's done. It's literally a detox for your environment, which has a great impact on your attitude and energy. Try to have an environmental detox item on your list of most important action items each day.

Forgiveness is a type of mental de-cluttering *detox*. Get those pent-up negative emotions and energies out of your life. Mad at yourself for letting your home get cluttered in the first place? Let it go, you're on the right path now even if you're managing the mess one small task at a time. Did your spouse overspend and rack-up huge credit card debt? Move on, the best thing you can do for that now is to forgive and find the solution (hello, manifest yourself the funds to pay off that debt) rather than dwelling in negative frustrations and memories. Try to truly forgive something or someone every single day.

Hanging on to negative events, memories, mistakes, debt, and heartache creates roadblocks to your success in manifesting abundance. When your mind is bogged down with the negatives, your predominant mental attitude is a negative one and you manifest negativity. It could be in the form of bad health, a speeding ticket, a surprise bill; and it all grew from a seed planted in your mind from a negative emotion.

Forgiveness is a detox for your mind. It's a choice to hold a grudge or hang on to the feeling of being a victim. Likewise, it's a choice to be strong and leave the past in the past. There's nothing you can do to change what has happened, but there is so much you can do to make a great today and tomorrow. Where do you really want to dwell, in a tough spot in your past or in the beautiful tomorrow you are now embarking on the journey to create?

Law of Attraction Lessons & Notes

There is so much to take in when you are learning how to use the Law of Attraction. Great quotes, great insight, great ideas, and general greatness that don't fit into the other categories need a place on your Golden Intuition workbook as well. Maybe you hear of a blog or author you'd like to check out, you see a great message on your Facebook feed, or maybe you just need an extra reminder to keep on the right path.

Are you ready?

Don't wait until tomorrow, next week, or until after some other event. Get started now. This workbook is personal and there are literally no wrong answers. Your time is now, let's get started!

A sample worksheet is included with some ideas to show you how to get started. Many of these ideas come right out of my personal notebook. The Law of Attraction is real, the energy in your body is real, so get ready for some real changes in your life.

Often when we start to truly change our vibrations and our lives, there is a bit of turbulence. Don't be surprised if there is some kick back. Stay strong, stay positive, and remember that bad days and bad moments are normal. We all have them, and now you are empowered with what you need to break out of that rut and soar into your dreams.

We all work at a different pace. Like most people, I had to start out small. My dreams stayed big, but my wants stayed small until I gained the confidence and experience in using the Law of Attraction to manifest amazing things in my life.

Should you ever get off track and miss a day, don't beat yourself up. Keep a positive mental attitude and pick up where you left off. It's always better to start from a step or two up than from the bottom.

Try to keep your journaling consistent, but most importantly keep a great mental attitude and allow yourself to use this guided planner as an opportunity to create the mental habits necessary to succeed with using the Law of Attraction to attract the life you desire.

"This is a great day and we are just getting started."

-Oprah

"The secret to getting ahead is getting started."

-Mark Twain

"What you to today can improve all your tomorrows."

-Ralph Marston

MPLE
ENTRY

Date: May 2, 2016

*"Worrying is using your imagination to
create something you don't want."*
-Abraham Hicks

Daily Intentions: Today I will have an amazingly wonderful day. I will show love to others and remember to think, feel, and act in line with my ambitions, desires, and intentions. I will keep focused & energetic.

Six Most Important Action Items Today:

1. Send out follow-up emails.
2. Work on 5-year business plan.
3. Go to the gym.
4. Schedule doctor's appointment.
5. Balance checking account.
6. Clean-out pantry.

I specifically want:

To Be...

Abundant in health, wealth, and happiness. Debt-free & RICH!

A top 25 successful real estate agent.

To Do...

Travel to Europe, pick my kids up from school every day, get manicures regularly.

To Have...

$100,000 in savings, a family, and a house in the hills with a pool.

How I will feel when I have it:

With money in the bank and a beautiful home to share with my family, I feel relaxed, happy, blissful, appreciative, full, and able to focus on myself and my family with my whole heart. I feel surrounded by abundance, fulfilled, and relaxed.

My Affirmations:

I am a debt-free millionaire.

I am so happy now that I make $20,000 each month.

I am healthy, wealthy, and wise.

I'm Grateful For:

1. The time I was able to spend with friends today.
2. The bonus I have coming at work.
3. The entertainment of cat on the internet.
4. The safe home I live in.
5. The beautiful weather this week.
6. WINE.

I Honestly Forgive:

My parents for passing down a negative attitude around money, my spouse for getting into debt, and myself for believing I am a victim.

Law of Attraction Lessons & Notes

- Your day-to-day life is someone else's dream life.

- Don't get attached to how the outcome will be achieved.

Date: _____

"The Mind moves in the direction of our currently dominant thoughts."

-Earl Nightingale

Daily Intentions: _____

_____

_____

_____

Six Most Important Action Items Today:

1. _____

2. _____

3. _____

4. _____

5. _____

6. _____

I specifically want:

To Be…

To Do...

To Have…

How I will feel when I have it:

My Affirmations:

I'm Grateful For:

1. _____
2. _____
3. _____
4. _____
5. _____
6. _____

I Honestly Forgive:

Law of Attraction Lessons & Notes:

Date: _____

*"The secret of success is
consistency of purpose."*

-Benjamin Disraeli

Daily Intentions: _____

_____

_____

_____

Six Most Important Action Items Today:

1. _____
2. _____
3. _____
4. _____
5. _____
6. _____

I specifically want:

To Be…

To Do...

To Have…

How I will feel when I have it:

My Affirmations:

I'm Grateful For:

1. _____
2. _____
3. _____
4. _____
5. _____
6. _____

I Honestly Forgive:

Law of Attraction Lessons & Notes:

Date: _____

"The best way to predict your future is to create it."
-Abraham Lincoln

Daily Intentions: _____

_____

_____

_____

Six Most Important Action Items Today:

1. _____
2. _____
3. _____
4. _____
5. _____
6. _____

I specifically want:

To Be…

To Do...

To Have…

How I will feel when I have it:

My Affirmations:

I'm Grateful For:

1. _____
2. _____
3. _____
4. _____
5. _____
6. _____

I Honestly Forgive:

Law of Attraction Lessons & Notes:

Date: _____

*"Sometimes it seems like getting the job is the hard part.
It never is. Doing a great job is always the greatest challenge."*
-Mark Cuban

Daily Intentions: _____

_____

_____

_____

Six Most Important Action Items Today:

1. _____
2. _____
3. _____
4. _____
5. _____
6. _____

I specifically want:

To Be…

To Do...

To Have…

How I will feel when I have it:

My Affirmations:

I'm Grateful For:

1. _____
2. _____
3. _____
4. _____
5. _____
6. _____

I Honestly Forgive:

Law of Attraction Lessons & Notes:

Date: _____

*"The best way to overcome undesirable or negative
thoughts and feelings is to cultivate positive ones."*
-William Walker Atkinson

Daily Intentions: _____

_____

_____

_____

Six Most Important Action Items Today:

1. _____
2. _____
3. _____
4. _____
5. _____
6. _____

I specifically want:

To Be…

To Do...

To Have…

How I will feel when I have it:

My Affirmations:

I'm Grateful For:

1. _____
2. _____
3. _____
4. _____
5. _____
6. _____

I Honestly Forgive:

Law of Attraction Lessons & Notes:

Date: _____

"Nothing can prevent your picture from coming into concrete form except the same power with which gave it birth – yourself."
-Genevieve Berhrend

Daily Intentions: _____

_____

_____

_____

Six Most Important Action Items Today:

1. _____
2. _____
3. _____
4. _____
5. _____
6. _____

I specifically want:

To Be…

To Do...

To Have…

How I will feel when I have it:

My Affirmations:

I'm Grateful For:

1. _____
2. _____
3. _____
4. _____
5. _____
6. _____

I Honestly Forgive:

Law of Attraction Lessons & Notes:

Date: _____

"What we are today comes from our thoughts of yesterday, and our present thoughts build our life of tomorrow: Our life is the creation of our mind."

-Buddha

Daily Intentions: _____

_____

_____

_____

Six Most Important Action Items Today:

1. _____
2. _____
3. _____
4. _____
5. _____
6. _____

I specifically want:

To Be…

To Do...

To Have…

How I will feel when I have it:

My Affirmations:

I'm Grateful For:

1. _____
2. _____
3. _____
4. _____
5. _____
6. _____

I Honestly Forgive:

Law of Attraction Lessons & Notes:

Date: _____

"The Law of Attraction states that whatever you focus on, think about, read about, and talk about intensely, you're going to attract more of into your life."

-Jack Canfield

Daily Intentions: _____

_____

_____

_____

Six Most Important Action Items Today:

1. _____

2. _____

3. _____

4. _____

5. _____

6. _____

I specifically want:

To Be…

To Do...

To Have…

How I will feel when I have it:

My Affirmations:

I'm Grateful For:

1. _____
2. _____
3. _____
4. _____
5. _____
6. _____

I Honestly Forgive:

Law of Attraction Lessons & Notes:

Date: _____

*"What you are is what you have been.
Who you will be is what you do now."*

-Buddha

Daily Intentions: _____

_____

_____

_____

Six Most Important Action Items Today:

1. _____
2. _____
3. _____
4. _____
5. _____
6. _____

I specifically want:

To Be…

To Do...

To Have…

How I will feel when I have it:

My Affirmations:

I'm Grateful For:

1. _____
2. _____
3. _____
4. _____
5. _____
6. _____

I Honestly Forgive:

Law of Attraction Lessons & Notes:

Date: _____

*"A man is but the product of his thoughts.
What he things he becomes."*

-Gandhi

Daily Intentions: _____

_____

_____

_____

Six Most Important Action Items Today:

1. _____
2. _____
3. _____
4. _____
5. _____
6. _____

I specifically want:

To Be…

To Do...

To Have…

How I will feel when I have it:

My Affirmations:

I'm Grateful For:

1. _____
2. _____
3. _____
4. _____
5. _____
6. _____

I Honestly Forgive:

Law of Attraction Lessons & Notes:

Date: _____

*"The vibrations of mental forces are the finest
and consequently the most powerful in existence."*
-Charles Haanel

Daily Intentions: _____

_____

_____

_____

Six Most Important Action Items Today:

1. _____
2. _____
3. _____
4. _____
5. _____
6. _____

I specifically want:

To Be…

To Do...

To Have…

How I will feel when I have it:

My Affirmations:

I'm Grateful For:

1. _____
2. _____
3. _____
4. _____
5. _____
6. _____

I Honestly Forgive:

Law of Attraction Lessons & Notes:

Date: _____

"Desire is the starting point of all achievement, not a hope, not a wish, but a keep pulsating desire which transcends everything."

-Napoleon Hill

Daily Intentions: _____

_____

_____

_____

Six Most Important Action Items Today:

1. _____
2. _____
3. _____
4. _____
5. _____
6. _____

I specifically want:

To Be…

To Do...

To Have…

How I will feel when I have it:

My Affirmations:

I'm Grateful For:

1. _____
2. _____
3. _____
4. _____
5. _____
6. _____

I Honestly Forgive:

Law of Attraction Lessons & Notes:

Date: _____

"The man who succeeds must always in mind or imagination live, move, think, and act as if he had gained that success, or he will never gain it."

-Prentice Mulford

Daily Intentions: _____

_____

_____

_____

Six Most Important Action Items Today:

1. _____
2. _____
3. _____
4. _____
5. _____
6. _____

I specifically want:

To Be…

To Do...

To Have…

How I will feel when I have it:

My Affirmations:

I'm Grateful For:

1. _____
2. _____
3. _____
4. _____
5. _____
6. _____

I Honestly Forgive:

Law of Attraction Lessons & Notes:

Date: _____

"Let's start with what we can be thankful for, and get our mind into that vibration, and then watch the good that starts to come, because one thought leads to another thought."

-Bob Proctor

Daily Intentions: _____

_____

_____

_____

Six Most Important Action Items Today:

1. _____
2. _____
3. _____
4. _____
5. _____
6. _____

I specifically want:

To Be…

To Do...

To Have…

How I will feel when I have it:

My Affirmations:

I'm Grateful For:

1. _____
2. _____
3. _____
4. _____
5. _____
6. _____

I Honestly Forgive:

Law of Attraction Lessons & Notes:

Date: _____

*"Music in the soul can
be heard by the universe."*

-Lao Tzu

Daily Intentions: _____

_____

_____

_____

Six Most Important Action Items Today:

1. _____
2. _____
3. _____
4. _____
5. _____
6. _____

I specifically want:

To Be…

To Do...

To Have…

How I will feel when I have it:

My Affirmations:

I'm Grateful For:

1. _____
2. _____
3. _____
4. _____
5. _____
6. _____

I Honestly Forgive:

Law of Attraction Lessons & Notes:

Date: _____

"As soon as you start to feel differently about what you already have, you will start to attract more of the good things, more of the things you can be grateful for."

-Joe Vitale

Daily Intentions: _____

_____

_____

_____

Six Most Important Action Items Today:

1. _____
2. _____
3. _____
4. _____
5. _____
6. _____

I specifically want:

To Be…

To Do...

To Have…

How I will feel when I have it:

My Affirmations:

I'm Grateful For:

1. _____
2. _____
3. _____
4. _____
5. _____
6. _____

I Honestly Forgive:

Law of Attraction Lessons & Notes:

Date: _____

*"The vibrations of mental forces are the finest
and consequently the most powerful in existence."*
-Charles Haanel

Daily Intentions: _____

_____

_____

_____

Six Most Important Action Items Today:

1. _____
2. _____
3. _____
4. _____
5. _____
6. _____

I specifically want:

To Be…

To Do...

To Have…

How I will feel when I have it:

My Affirmations:

I'm Grateful For:

1. _____
2. _____
3. _____
4. _____
5. _____
6. _____

I Honestly Forgive:

Law of Attraction Lessons & Notes:

Date: _____

*"You are to become a creator, not a competitor; you are
going to get what you want, but in such a way that when you
get it every other man will have more than he has now."*
                                                -Wallace D. Wattles

Daily Intentions: _____

_____

_____

_____

Six Most Important Action Items Today:

1. _____
2. _____
3. _____
4. _____
5. _____
6. _____

I specifically want:

To Be…

To Do...

To Have…

How I will feel when I have it:

My Affirmations:

I'm Grateful For:

1. _____
2. _____
3. _____
4. _____
5. _____
6. _____

I Honestly Forgive:

Law of Attraction Lessons & Notes:

Date: _____

"The use of the will as the projector of mentative
currents is the real base of all mental magic."
-William Walker Atkinson

Daily Intentions: _____

_____

_____

_____

Six Most Important Action Items Today:

1. _____
2. _____
3. _____
4. _____
5. _____
6. _____

I specifically want:

To Be…

To Do…

To Have…

How I will feel when I have it:

My Affirmations:

I'm Grateful For:

1. _____
2. _____
3. _____
4. _____
5. _____
6. _____

I Honestly Forgive:

Law of Attraction Lessons & Notes:

Date: _____

*"Everyone visualizes whether he knows it or not.
Visualizing is the great secret of success."*
-Genevieve Berhrend

Daily Intentions: _____

_____

_____

_____

Six Most Important Action Items Today:

1. _____
2. _____
3. _____
4. _____
5. _____
6. _____

I specifically want:

To Be…

To Do...

To Have…

How I will feel when I have it:

My Affirmations:

I'm Grateful For:

1. _____
2. _____
3. _____
4. _____
5. _____
6. _____

I Honestly Forgive:

Law of Attraction Lessons & Notes:

Date: _____

"Everything you want is out there waiting for you to ask. Everything you want also wants you.
But you have to take action to get it.."

-Jack Canfield

Daily Intentions: _____

_____

_____

_____

Six Most Important Action Items Today:

1. _____

2. _____

3. _____

4. _____

5. _____

6. _____

I specifically want:

To Be…

To Do...

To Have…

How I will feel when I have it:

My Affirmations:

I'm Grateful For:

1. _____
2. _____
3. _____
4. _____
5. _____
6. _____

I Honestly Forgive:

Law of Attraction Lessons & Notes:

Date: _____

*"There is no limit to what this law can do for you;
dare to believe in your own idea; think of the
ideal as an already accomplished fact."*

-Charles Haanel

Daily Intentions: _____

_____

_____

_____

Six Most Important Action Items Today:

1. _____
2. _____
3. _____
4. _____
5. _____
6. _____

I specifically want:

To Be...

To Do...

To Have...

How I will feel when I have it:

My Affirmations:

I'm Grateful For:

1. _____
2. _____
3. _____
4. _____
5. _____
6. _____

I Honestly Forgive:

Law of Attraction Lessons & Notes:

Date: _____

*"Man, alone, has the power to transform his
thoughts into physical reality; man alone, can
dream and make his dreams come true."*

-Napoleon Hill

Daily Intentions: _____

_____

_____

_____

Six Most Important Action Items Today:

1. _____
2. _____
3. _____
4. _____
5. _____
6. _____

I specifically want:

To Be…

To Do...

To Have…

How I will feel when I have it:

My Affirmations:

I'm Grateful For:

1. _____
2. _____
3. _____
4. _____
5. _____
6. _____

I Honestly Forgive:

Law of Attraction Lessons & Notes:

Date: _____

"Our thought is the unseen magnet, ever attracting its correspondence in things seen and tangible."

-*Prentice Mulford*

Daily Intentions: _____

_____

_____

_____

Six Most Important Action Items Today:

1. _____
2. _____
3. _____
4. _____
5. _____
6. _____

I specifically want:

To Be…

To Do...

To Have…

How I will feel when I have it:

My Affirmations:

I'm Grateful For:

1. _____
2. _____
3. _____
4. _____
5. _____
6. _____

I Honestly Forgive:

Law of Attraction Lessons & Notes:

LAW OF ATTRACTION DAILY WORKBOOK & PLANNER

Date: _____

*"Thoughts are sending out that magnetic
signal that is drawing the parallel back to you."*

-*Joe Vitale*

Daily Intentions: _____

_____

_____

_____

Six Most Important Action Items Today:

1. _____
2. _____
3. _____
4. _____
5. _____
6. _____

I specifically want:

To Be…

To Do...

To Have…

How I will feel when I have it:

My Affirmations:

I'm Grateful For:

1. _____
2. _____
3. _____
4. _____
5. _____
6. _____

I Honestly Forgive:

Law of Attraction Lessons & Notes:

Date: _____

"By thought, the thing you want is brought to you.
By action, you receive it."

-Wallace D. Wattles

Daily Intentions: _____

_____

_____

_____

Six Most Important Action Items Today:

1. _____
2. _____
3. _____
4. _____
5. _____
6. _____

I specifically want:

To Be...

To Do...

To Have...

How I will feel when I have it:

My Affirmations:

I'm Grateful For:

1. _____
2. _____
3. _____
4. _____
5. _____
6. _____

I Honestly Forgive:

Law of Attraction Lessons & Notes:

Date: _____

"Cherish your visions and your dreams as they are the children of your soul, the blueprints of your ultimate achievements."

-Napoleon Hill

Daily Intentions: _____

_____

_____

_____

Six Most Important Action Items Today:

1. _____
2. _____
3. _____
4. _____
5. _____
6. _____

I specifically want:

To Be…

To Do...

To Have…

How I will feel when I have it:

My Affirmations:

I'm Grateful For:

1. _____
2. _____
3. _____
4. _____
5. _____
6. _____

I Honestly Forgive:

Law of Attraction Lessons & Notes:

Date: _____

*"Trade your expectation for appreciation
and the world changes instantly."*

-Tony Robbins

Daily Intentions: _____

_____

_____

_____

Six Most Important Action Items Today:

1. _____

2. _____

3. _____

4. _____

5. _____

6. _____

I specifically want:

To Be…

To Do...

To Have…

How I will feel when I have it:

My Affirmations:

I'm Grateful For:

1. _____
2. _____
3. _____
4. _____
5. _____
6. _____

I Honestly Forgive:

Law of Attraction Lessons & Notes:

Date: _____

*"Life will give you whatever experience is most
helpful for the evolution of your consciousness."*

-Eckhard Tolle

Daily Intentions: _____

_____

_____

_____

Six Most Important Action Items Today:

1. _____

2. _____

3. _____

4. _____

5. _____

6. _____

I specifically want:

To Be…

To Do...

To Have…

How I will feel when I have it:

My Affirmations:

I'm Grateful For:

1. _____
2. _____
3. _____
4. _____
5. _____
6. _____

I Honestly Forgive:

Law of Attraction Lessons & Notes:

Date: _____

"The secret to success is consistency of purpose."
-Benjamin Disraeli

Daily Intentions: _____

_____

_____

_____

Six Most Important Action Items Today:

1. _____
2. _____
3. _____
4. _____
5. _____
6. _____

I specifically want:

To Be…

To Do...

To Have…

How I will feel when I have it:

My Affirmations:

I'm Grateful For:

1. _____
2. _____
3. _____
4. _____
5. _____
6. _____

I Honestly Forgive:

Law of Attraction Lessons & Notes:

Date: _____

*"The way the Universe works is quite simple – you have
a desire, and it is always answered, every single time."*

-Abraham Hicks

Daily Intentions: _____

_____

_____

_____

Six Most Important Action Items Today:

1. _____
2. _____
3. _____
4. _____
5. _____
6. _____

I specifically want:

To Be…

To Do...

To Have…

How I will feel when I have it:

My Affirmations:

I'm Grateful For:

1. _____
2. _____
3. _____
4. _____
5. _____
6. _____

I Honestly Forgive:

Law of Attraction Lessons & Notes:

Date: _____

*"We all know that a rocket burns most of its fuel during
the first few moments of flight as it overcomes inertia
and the gravitational pull of the earth. That's what it's like for
us as we launch our dreams into physical reality."*

-Maria Nemeth, PHD

Daily Intentions: _____

_____

_____

_____

Six Most Important Action Items Today:

1. _____
2. _____
3. _____
4. _____
5. _____
6. _____

I specifically want:

To Be…

To Do...

To Have…

How I will feel when I have it:

My Affirmations:

I'm Grateful For:

1. _____
2. _____
3. _____
4. _____
5. _____
6. _____

I Honestly Forgive:

Law of Attraction Lessons & Notes:

Date: _____

"You'll see it when you believe it."

-Dr. Wayne Dyer

Daily Intentions: _____

_____

_____

_____

Six Most Important Action Items Today:

1. _____
2. _____
3. _____
4. _____
5. _____
6. _____

I specifically want:

To Be…

To Do...

To Have…

How I will feel when I have it:

My Affirmations:

I'm Grateful For:

1. _____
2. _____
3. _____
4. _____
5. _____
6. _____

I Honestly Forgive:

Law of Attraction Lessons & Notes:

Date: _____

"Formal education will make you a living;
self-education will make you a fortune."

-Jim Rohn

Daily Intentions: _____

_____

_____

_____

Six Most Important Action Items Today:

1. _____
2. _____
3. _____
4. _____
5. _____
6. _____

I specifically want:

To Be…

To Do...

To Have…

How I will feel when I have it:

My Affirmations:

I'm Grateful For:

1. _____
2. _____
3. _____
4. _____
5. _____
6. _____

I Honestly Forgive:

Law of Attraction Lessons & Notes:

Date: _____

*"Happiness doesn't just flow from success;
it actually causes it."*

-Richard Wiseman

Daily Intentions: _____

_____

_____

_____

Six Most Important Action Items Today:

1. _____
2. _____
3. _____
4. _____
5. _____
6. _____

I specifically want:

To Be…

To Do...

To Have…

How I will feel when I have it:

My Affirmations:

I'm Grateful For:

1. _____
2. _____
3. _____
4. _____
5. _____
6. _____

I Honestly Forgive:

Law of Attraction Lessons & Notes:

Date: _____

"When riches begin to come, they come so quickly and in such great abundance that one wonders where they have been hiding during all those lean years."

-Napoleon Hill

Daily Intentions: _____

_____

_____

_____

Six Most Important Action Items Today:

1. _____
2. _____
3. _____
4. _____
5. _____
6. _____

I specifically want:

To Be…

To Do...

To Have…

How I will feel when I have it:

My Affirmations:

I'm Grateful For:

1. _____
2. _____
3. _____
4. _____
5. _____
6. _____

I Honestly Forgive:

Law of Attraction Lessons & Notes:

Date: _____

*"Money Conciousness means that the mind has become
so thoroughly saturated with the desire for money that
one can see one's self already in possession of it."*
-Napoleon Hill

Daily Intentions: _____

_____

_____

_____

Six Most Important Action Items Today:

1. _____
2. _____
3. _____
4. _____
5. _____
6. _____

I specifically want:

To Be…

To Do…

To Have…

How I will feel when I have it:

My Affirmations:

I'm Grateful For:

1. _____
2. _____
3. _____
4. _____
5. _____
6. _____

I Honestly Forgive:

Law of Attraction Lessons & Notes:

Date: _____

"Your imagination is your preview of life's coming attractions."
-Albert Einstein

Daily Intentions: _____

_____

_____

_____

Six Most Important Action Items Today:

1. _____
2. _____
3. _____
4. _____
5. _____
6. _____

I specifically want:

To Be…

To Do...

To Have…

How I will feel when I have it:

My Affirmations:

I'm Grateful For:

1. _____
2. _____
3. _____
4. _____
5. _____
6. _____

I Honestly Forgive:

Law of Attraction Lessons & Notes:

Date: _____

"Every single second is an opportunity to change your life, because in any moment you can change the way you feel."
                                                    -Rhonda Byrne

Daily Intentions: _____

_____

_____

_____

Six Most Important Action Items Today:

1. _____
2. _____
3. _____
4. _____
5. _____
6. _____

I specifically want:

To Be…

To Do...

To Have…

How I will feel when I have it:

My Affirmations:

I'm Grateful For:

1. _____
2. _____
3. _____
4. _____
5. _____
6. _____

I Honestly Forgive:

Law of Attraction Lessons & Notes:

Date: _____

*"Whether you think you can or think you can't,
either way you are always right."*

-*Henry Ford*

Daily Intentions: _____

_____

_____

_____

Six Most Important Action Items Today:

1. _____
2. _____
3. _____
4. _____
5. _____
6. _____

I specifically want:

To Be…

To Do...

To Have…

How I will feel when I have it:

My Affirmations:

I'm Grateful For:

1. _____
2. _____
3. _____
4. _____
5. _____
6. _____

I Honestly Forgive:

Law of Attraction Lessons & Notes:

Date: _____

"Nothing external to me has any power over me."
-Walt Whitman

Daily Intentions: _____

_____

_____

_____

Six Most Important Action Items Today:

1. _____
2. _____
3. _____
4. _____
5. _____
6. _____

I specifically want:

To Be…

To Do...

To Have…

How I will feel when I have it:

My Affirmations:

I'm Grateful For:

1. _____
2. _____
3. _____
4. _____
5. _____
6. _____

I Honestly Forgive:

Law of Attraction Lessons & Notes:

Date: _____

"Happiness is not a destination.
It is a method of life."

-Burton Hills

Daily Intentions: _____

_____

_____

_____

Six Most Important Action Items Today:

1. _____

2. _____

3. _____

4. _____

5. _____

6. _____

I specifically want:

To Be…

To Do...

To Have…

How I will feel when I have it:

My Affirmations:

I'm Grateful For:

1. _____
2. _____
3. _____
4. _____
5. _____
6. _____

I Honestly Forgive:

Law of Attraction Lessons & Notes:

Date: _____

"To bring anything in your life, imagine that it's already there."
-Richard Back

Daily Intentions: _____

_____

_____

_____

Six Most Important Action Items Today:

1. _____
2. _____
3. _____
4. _____
5. _____
6. _____

I specifically want:

To Be…

To Do...

To Have…

How I will feel when I have it:

My Affirmations:

I'm Grateful For:

1. _____
2. _____
3. _____
4. _____
5. _____
6. _____

I Honestly Forgive:

Law of Attraction Lessons & Notes:

Date: _____

*"The only person you are destined to become is…
the person you decide to be."*
-Ralph Waldo Emerson

Daily Intentions: _____

_____

_____

_____

Six Most Important Action Items Today:

1. _____
2. _____
3. _____
4. _____
5. _____
6. _____

I specifically want:

To Be…

To Do...

To Have…

How I will feel when I have it:

My Affirmations:

I'm Grateful For:

1. _____
2. _____
3. _____
4. _____
5. _____
6. _____

I Honestly Forgive:

Law of Attraction Lessons & Notes:

Date: _____

"Your thoughts are the architects of your destiny."
                                    -David O. McKay

Daily Intentions: _____

_____

_____

_____

Six Most Important Action Items Today:

1. _____
2. _____
3. _____
4. _____
5. _____
6. _____

I specifically want:

To Be…

To Do...

To Have…

How I will feel when I have it:

My Affirmations:

I'm Grateful For:

1. _____
2. _____
3. _____
4. _____
5. _____
6. _____

I Honestly Forgive:

Law of Attraction Lessons & Notes:

Date: _____

"Nothing is impossible, the word itself says 'I'm Possible'."
                                                    -Audrey Hepburn

Daily Intentions: _____

_____

_____

_____

Six Most Important Action Items Today:

1. _____
2. _____
3. _____
4. _____
5. _____
6. _____

I specifically want:

To Be…

To Do...

To Have…

How I will feel when I have it:

My Affirmations:

I'm Grateful For:

1. _____
2. _____
3. _____
4. _____
5. _____
6. _____

I Honestly Forgive:

Law of Attraction Lessons & Notes:

Date: _____

"We receive exactly what we expect to receive."
-John Holland

Daily Intentions: _____

_____

_____

_____

Six Most Important Action Items Today:

1. _____
2. _____
3. _____
4. _____
5. _____
6. _____

I specifically want:

To Be…

To Do...

To Have…

How I will feel when I have it:

My Affirmations:

I'm Grateful For:

1. _____
2. _____
3. _____
4. _____
5. _____
6. _____

I Honestly Forgive:

Law of Attraction Lessons & Notes:

Date: _____

"Be thankful for what you have; you'll end up having more. If you concentrate on what you don't have you, will never ever have enough."

-Oprah Winfrey

Daily Intentions: _____

_____

_____

_____

Six Most Important Action Items Today:

1. _____
2. _____
3. _____
4. _____
5. _____
6. _____

I specifically want:

To Be…

To Do...

To Have…

How I will feel when I have it:

My Affirmations:

I'm Grateful For:

1. _____
2. _____
3. _____
4. _____
5. _____
6. _____

I Honestly Forgive:

Law of Attraction Lessons & Notes:

Date: _____

"Edison failed 10,000 times before he made the electric light.
Do not be discouraged if you fail a few times."

-Napoleon Hill

Daily Intentions: _____

_____

_____

_____

Six Most Important Action Items Today:

1. _____
2. _____
3. _____
4. _____
5. _____
6. _____

I specifically want:

To Be…

To Do...

To Have…

How I will feel when I have it:

My Affirmations:

I'm Grateful For:

1. _____
2. _____
3. _____
4. _____
5. _____
6. _____

I Honestly Forgive:

Law of Attraction Lessons & Notes:

Date: _____

*"Set a goal to achieve something so big, so exhilarating
that it excites you and scares you at the same time."*

-Bob Proctor

Daily Intentions: _____

_____

_____

_____

Six Most Important Action Items Today:

1. _____
2. _____
3. _____
4. _____
5. _____
6. _____

I specifically want:

To Be…

To Do...

To Have…

How I will feel when I have it:

My Affirmations:

I'm Grateful For:

1. _____
2. _____
3. _____
4. _____
5. _____
6. _____

I Honestly Forgive:

Law of Attraction Lessons & Notes:

Date: _____

*"You create your thoughts, your thoughts create
your intentions, and your intentions create your reality."*
-Wayne Dyer

Daily Intentions: _____

_____

_____

_____

Six Most Important Action Items Today:

1. _____
2. _____
3. _____
4. _____
5. _____
6. _____

I specifically want:

To Be…

To Do...

To Have…

How I will feel when I have it:

My Affirmations:

I'm Grateful For:

1. _____
2. _____
3. _____
4. _____
5. _____
6. _____

I Honestly Forgive:

Law of Attraction Lessons & Notes:

Date: _____

"Ask for what you want and be prepared to get it!"
-Maya Angelou

Daily Intentions: _____

_____

_____

_____

Six Most Important Action Items Today:

1. _____
2. _____
3. _____
4. _____
5. _____
6. _____

I specifically want:

To Be...

To Do...

To Have...

How I will feel when I have it:

My Affirmations:

I'm Grateful For:

1. _____
2. _____
3. _____
4. _____
5. _____
6. _____

I Honestly Forgive:

Law of Attraction Lessons & Notes:

Date: _____

*"Follow your bliss and the Universe will
open doors where there were walls."*
-Joseph Campbell

Daily Intentions: _____

_____

_____

_____

Six Most Important Action Items Today:

1. _____
2. _____
3. _____
4. _____
5. _____
6. _____

I specifically want:

To Be…

To Do...

To Have…

How I will feel when I have it:

My Affirmations:

I'm Grateful For:

1. _____
2. _____
3. _____
4. _____
5. _____
6. _____

I Honestly Forgive:

Law of Attraction Lessons & Notes:

Date: _____

"Change your thoughts and you change your world."
-Norman Vincent Peale

Daily Intentions: _____

_____

_____

_____

Six Most Important Action Items Today:

1. _____
2. _____
3. _____
4. _____
5. _____
6. _____

I specifically want:

To Be…

To Do...

To Have…

How I will feel when I have it:

My Affirmations:

I'm Grateful For:

1. _____
2. _____
3. _____
4. _____
5. _____
6. _____

I Honestly Forgive:

Law of Attraction Lessons & Notes:

Date: _____

*"Once you replace negative thoughts with positive
ones, you'll start having positive results."*

-Willie Nelson

Daily Intentions: _____

_____

_____

_____

Six Most Important Action Items Today:

1. _____
2. _____
3. _____
4. _____
5. _____
6. _____

I specifically want:

To Be…

To Do...

To Have…

How I will feel when I have it:

My Affirmations:

I'm Grateful For:

1. _____
2. _____
3. _____
4. _____
5. _____
6. _____

I Honestly Forgive:

Law of Attraction Lessons & Notes:

Date: _____

"Be very careful what you set your heart
upon, for you will surely have it."
-*Ralph Waldo Emerson*

Daily Intentions: _____

_____

_____

_____

Six Most Important Action Items Today:

1. _____
2. _____
3. _____
4. _____
5. _____
6. _____

I specifically want:

To Be…

To Do...

To Have…

How I will feel when I have it:

My Affirmations:

I'm Grateful For:

1. _____
2. _____
3. _____
4. _____
5. _____
6. _____

I Honestly Forgive:

Law of Attraction Lessons & Notes:

Date: _____

"The better you feel, the more you allow."

-Abraham Hicks

Daily Intentions: _____

_____

_____

_____

Six Most Important Action Items Today:

1. _____
2. _____
3. _____
4. _____
5. _____
6. _____

I specifically want:

To Be…

To Do…

To Have…

How I will feel when I have it:

My Affirmations:

I'm Grateful For:

1. _____
2. _____
3. _____
4. _____
5. _____
6. _____

I Honestly Forgive:

Law of Attraction Lessons & Notes:

Date: _____

"It's our intention. Our intention is everything. Nothing happens on this planet without it. Not one single thing has ever been accomplished without intention."

-Jim Carrey

Daily Intentions: _____

_____

_____

_____

Six Most Important Action Items Today:

1. _____
2. _____
3. _____
4. _____
5. _____
6. _____

I specifically want:

To Be…

To Do...

To Have…

How I will feel when I have it:

My Affirmations:

I'm Grateful For:

1. _____
2. _____
3. _____
4. _____
5. _____
6. _____

I Honestly Forgive:

Law of Attraction Lessons & Notes:

Date: _____

"Whatever the mind can conceive it can achieve."
-W. Clenent Stone

Daily Intentions: _____

_____

_____

_____

Six Most Important Action Items Today:

1. _____
2. _____
3. _____
4. _____
5. _____
6. _____

I specifically want:

To Be…

To Do...

To Have…

How I will feel when I have it:

My Affirmations:

I'm Grateful For:

1. _____
2. _____
3. _____
4. _____
5. _____
6. _____

I Honestly Forgive:

Law of Attraction Lessons & Notes:

Date: _____

"The greatest discovery of my generation is that a human being can alter his life by altering his attitudes of mind."

-William James

Daily Intentions: _____

_____

_____

_____

Six Most Important Action Items Today:

1. _____
2. _____
3. _____
4. _____
5. _____
6. _____

I specifically want:

To Be…

To Do...

To Have…

How I will feel when I have it:

My Affirmations:

I'm Grateful For:

1. _____
2. _____
3. _____
4. _____
5. _____
6. _____

I Honestly Forgive:

Law of Attraction Lessons & Notes:

Congratulations!

How has your life changed in the past 60 days? Have you finally begun to use your mind like a master manifestor?

Don't worry if you haven't seen everything just yet. It's coming! Now is your time. The Universe is aligning to your new, improved vibration. What you've been dreaming, feeling, and acting on is creating wonderful things for you. You've been letting go of old, negative thoughts and habits while creating the new ones you'll need to receive.

Take Note of What Has Changed

We all respond to changes at different paces. Think about where your life was when you began by looking back at your first entries. What victories have you had in your life & career (both big & small). How can you fine-tune what you are receiving by asking in a more specific way?

When I first became a great manifestor, I set my intentions on a new, white 7-seater SUV and a Rolex. In a freak accident, my car was totaled and my arm went through the window destroying my watch. My settlement more than paid for the new, dream car (which happened to be sitting at the dealership in the color & configuration I wanted *on sale* that week) and Rolex, but I could have done without the pain and stress from an auto accident. You may also have learned some lessons on being more specific and feeling more comfortable asking, expecting, believing, and receiving. This book was developed in response to this need and I intend to continue to offer more ways to help others be their own successful creators with additional workbooks & planners.

Keep Going!

If you'd like to keep improving your life, vibrations, and abilities to manifest your dreams through the Law of Attraction, pick up another copy of this planner or see other offerings from Aria Edwards.

70963536R00077

Made in the USA
Columbia, SC
19 May 2017